Chips, Paracetamol and Wine

Graham Fulton

STACK BOOKS

Smokestack Books
1 Lake Terrace, Grewelthorpe,
Ripon HG4 3BU
e-mail: info@smokestack-books.co.uk
www.smokestack-books.co.uk

Poems copyright
Graham Fulton, 2020,
all rights reserved.

ISBN 9781916312135

Smokestack Books
is represented by
Inpress Ltd

Chips, Paracetamol and Wine

*for Helen,
again*

Contents

a man made of chips
Book Terrorist	13
Ricky the Dunderheid	14
Rascal	15
Peripheral	16
Bring Me the Head of John Logie Baird	18
Titan	19
The Kromer Hat Statue in Clydebank	21
Theoretical	23
Golden Stream of Poetry	24
The Institute Babies	25
The Mystery of the Vanishing Barber	26
Unusual Suspects	27
The Eternal Co-op	28
Brian Wilson in Morrisons	29
Stuffed	30
The Poetry Reaper	32
Charles the Third	34
The Great Glasgow Science Tower Disaster	36
Kylie's Pants are Calling Me	37
He's Behind You	41
Beautiful	43
The Three Junkies	44
The Three Dancers	45

a man made of paracetamol
Big Bang	49
The Moons of Uranus	50
Young Disciples	52
Unclean	53
The Lanes	54
The Postman	55
Freaks	56
Hatrack Monsters	57
The Details	58

International Brigade Statue on Custom House Quay	60
The Muppet Show	61
Techno Tin Bin Man	63
Flaw of Nature	64
Unfathomable	65
Marcelitis and Other Diseases	66
Daily Planet	68
A Fly	69
Bowel Screening Test	71
A Clockwork Nokia	72
Reptile House	74
Reptilius Completelymentalus	75
Unexpect the Expected	77
The Pedestrian Crossing Light Bulb Changer	79
The Lights	80
Earth on Heaven	81
All Yesterday's Parties	82

a man made of wine

Whatever You Do Don't Smile	85
Parking Meter	86
Memento Mori	88
Tom Leonard's Funeral	89
The Cockett Cats	90
The Projector's Broken and is Never Going to be Fixed	92
Beat Poem	94
Jimmy Johnstone	96
Davie Cooper	98
Cathkin Park	100
There Was Once a Moment When None of This Existed	102
Set the Controls for the Heart of The Club Bar in Paisley	104
Empty Fairground	105
Inflation	107
Parallel	108
The Toothpaste Cage	109
The Cork Jugs	111
The Choir Windows of Dunblane Cathedral	112
The Shed Man	114

Post Office Masks	116
Toddlers in the Park	117
An Idiot	118
Confess	120
Chips, Paracetamol and Wine	122
Stop	124
Acknowledgements	125

**a man
made
of chips**

Book Terrorist

I put books on the shelves
of bookshops when no one
is looking

when the assistant
is eagerly stacking
the creaking wood
with celebrity memoirs

I lift them out of
my book bag

slide them into
the right place

leave,
slowly

I don't want money

Someone someday
might find one
and take it to
the counter and say
Dear Mr and Mrs Bookshop
how much is this excellently dusty
slim volume of slim verse?

and they won't know,
or how it got there

Ricky the Dunderheid

Ricky the dunderheid
has been putting all of the right mail
into all of the wrong letterboxes
with a cheery smile on his face
and a low intelligence quotient
in his brain
according to his superior postman
who told me *Ricky's a pure dunderheid,*
av telt im time an time again
tay check thi names on thi doors
but he's thick as mince,
and there are people
opening telephone bills and electricity bills
and threatening letters from debt collectors
and love letters
and hate letters
and the latest copy of *Poets' Wives*
and the latest copy of *Shit Science*
and the pricelist for *Little Psychopaths' Nursery*
that should have been delivered
to different inhabitants,
and it's happening so much
people are doubting
who they are and what their names are
and wondering if all their precious memories
of childhood and dead parents
and foreign wars you can't possibly win
have been artificially inserted
into their minds,
and if they are in fact Mrs Mussolini
from the next block,
or Mrs McGlumphit from the top floor,
or Mr Plott from the ground floor,
except for the ones who get no mail
at all like us who have always known
that we don't exist

Rascal

stuck to a post with silver tape
is a notice asking
if we've seen
Rascal
the cat
who's micro-chipped and neutered
and marked in black and white
and been missing from home
since August,
it's December,
I reckon
Rascal is toast
and it's begging anyone, me, us,
to look in sheds and foliage
in case he's injured or frightened
and I can feel their love
but it's too long
he's probably
up in pussy heaven
with his pussy pals
and no one is going to collect
the £250 reward

and the rain of months
has cancered inside
the plastic pocket,
the once clean photograph
of *Rascal*'s black and white islands
has come alive and stained into
an unshaped dream,
it hurts
to see him this way,
it hurts I'll never know
what happened to *Rascal*, me,
anyone, you, it cuts my heart

Peripheral

There's a kissing couple
        in the left hand corner
of the red brick shelter
            in the park as I pass. I can
hear the sound
        of lips smacking and slurping
and tongues writhing
            and coiling over and
over like eels
        in a basin.
I can

identify a white blur
            which could be a human shirt
from the furthest corner
        of my left eye
but can't tell if it's
            a boy or a girl or what
the other person is, I daren't
        turn and look in case
they stop and stare or even
            chase after me saying things like
Whiddyi think yur lookin at
        ya park-strollin pervert?
or even
        creatively slice off my penis
with an eight inch blade.
Maybe

                        it's only one person
honing his love-making techniques
                        for future use
with his own lonely arms cuddling
            his own back and his own tongue
going in and out of
            the mouth-shaped hole he's created
with his thumb and first finger, it could
            very well be that.
I have

            nothing
to go on, nothing except the noises,
                        only
the noises.

Bring Me the Head of John Logie Baird

Mr Watson   Come here   I want to see you
were the first words spoken
by Alexander Graham Bell
right after he'd invented
the easy payment swipe screen smart phone
with full infinity access to hardcore pornography,
but as there's no statue of him in Scotland
I'll go to see the bust of John Logie Baird instead
who invented the 90 inch ceiling-dangling
fibre optic high definition controlled-by-a-chip-
inserted-in-your-brain-at-birth television
in Helensburgh,
but he's in a right state
as they're removing the esplanade
to make way for a crazy golf course
designed by Charles Rennie Mackintosh,
and all that's left of his pioneering spectacles
is the bridge welded to his nose
because maybe he's been watching
too much telly.
and it appears he's had his fill of modern life,
the choices, the unlimitations,
but seems quite content
as he gazes chubbily out
over the low tide Clyde
with only the no-nonsense clouds
moving unhurriedly from right to left,
the big sun coming and going,
and the mad gulls bouncing from clump to clump
of brown seaweed which looks like billions
of the top halves of hairy human heads
with the rest of the body submerged
and no way to change the channel.

Titan

Young men attached to cords
                launch themselves from the top
      of the big blue crane in Clydebank
                as women and children whoop
and clap.
People in the gift shop are buying
                key rings, pencils,
                    erasers, sharpeners,
and books of poetry by Brian Whittingham,
or watching films
        of funnels, platers, joiners, carpenters,
                workers wearing masks,
lumps of grey chain being dragged
                      along a slipway
as the guide tells us
there are half a million rivets holding
                    it all together,
        and if we look to the left we can see
              where the sheds used to stand,
  with the clouds and the sun and the cantilever steel
               and a plane to the Emirates
reflected in the oily water,
                hard and black,
patiently calm,
        except for the parts where it looks as if
            it's been brushed by the back
of an invisible hand.

Dandelion clocks
are sailing on the air,
            charting their courses,
                  welding to my eyes.

A photograph of flat-capped phantoms
                       stretches the length
of a chain-link fence.

The people down there
look just like dolls.

As I'm coming back in the lift
                 a bungee jumper tells me
                             it felt like it must feel
     when you've just given birth,
but there's no way
               he'll say that to his wife.

He likes being alive too much.

The Kromer Hat Statue in Clydebank

is splatted with
the compulsory bird keech

dribbled and dried
on the roof of his head.

He looks like
a computer generated
identikit warrior

or a holyman,
with his chiselled jaw
and lethal cheeks

aiming towards the Clyde,
somewhere beyond
the traffic lights.

His girder plinth
is islanded with rust,
the title plate
is long removed

unscrewed
for scrap.

Molten words.

Perhaps it's designed
to be like this,
an invitation to the future,
a defiance of the past

the hero welder
from an epic poem

a backward cap from Milwaukee
on his head,
the symbol for something
carved into his chest.

He seems comfortable
in his bronze

keeping his lips sealed
about everything best left
unsaid.

Theoretical

a man in the bus stop
is writing in the air
with the pointing finger
                       of his right hand

making elaborate squiggles
and patterns
until his number comes
                       and he goes

maybe
it was his shopping list
                       maybe
he's a
mentalist

or maybe
it was a brand new equation
for what created the Higgs Boson particle
which binds us all together

$y+v = m$

your vacuum
                       is as good
as mine

Golden Stream of Poetry

a nice brown dog
               in a nice red coat
is recorded in
          the function of urinating
against the statue
              of nature lover
and dead poet
                Alexander Wilson
outside
     Paisley Town Hall
at precisely
          10.36 a.m.
in the passing rain
             as his master
in a black anorak
               and black beanie hat
       watches
and waits

The Institute Babies

2014

clawed and chewed,
veined with droppings,
the seven bronze statues
in the niches on the walls
of the Russell Institute
for Children's Welfare
in Paisley
are still
maintaining
the dead benefactor's faith
in old fashioned things
like compassion and hope,
with two naked
well fed green weans
moaning in pain
at their toothache faces,
two more wincing
at their bandaged fingers,
and one raising his healing foot,
and one squealing with delight
at his new pair of specs, and one
looking down in confusion
at the space where
his new pair of specs should be,
broken long ago,
next to
the glorious-faced angel of mercy
holding out a bowl of plenty
above the boarded-up door
of the derelict shell

The Mystery of the Vanishing Barber

here's my barber
from the *Aff Yer Heid* Gents,
who never speaks, especially when spoken to,
turning left into a doorway
which, because of the angle, looks totally
one dimensional, flat, on the edge
of disappearing   and I can't tell
if it's the bakers or the bookies
or the funeral home, and because
I'm looking over my shoulder
and moving further away all the time
with each step
I'll never know
what he likes to do
with his lunch break   whether it's
choosing a sandwich, placing a bet on an animal,
selecting a tasteful monumental urn
for a customer, recently deceased.
and he must have gone right past me
without perceiving, or caring,
even though he cut my hair 15 minutes before
for nine quid   including a tip   as if
I'm not really there, as if everything concerned
with things that grow, are cut, swept
and binned, are not a part of life or death.

Unusual Suspects

5 policemen
stroll into the Sherwood chippy
with bulging manly black pockets
and *Z Cars* hats
and walkie talkies
and cuffs
and keys
and various
tools of natural enforcement
around their drug-busting waists
politely order
3 fish suppers
and 2 black pudding suppers
lavished with salt
and vinegar
and five cans of *Irn-Bru*
and pickled onions from a jar
like real human beings
with normal appetites
as we
who were here first
stand in a line against the back wall
trying not to make eye contact
and looking as guilty as hell
of crimes against cholesterol

The Eternal Co-op

On the way there
a man slips
a piece of paper
into my hand
that asks
Where Will You Spend Eternity?

It makes me think.
I'm not too sure.

On the way back
with my low calorie tonic
he tries to
give me another
but stops in time
while saying
I've given you one already!

Haven't I?

Indeed you have.
And now I know.

One eternity
is more than enough.

Brian Wilson in Morrisons

an old man wearing
a black I LOVE LA
baseball cap

is slowly scanning
a monster box
of KARCHER K2
PRESSURE WASHER

while whistling
I Get Around
by The Beach Boys

Stuffed

A Yorkshire Toy King Terrier
is in Paisley Museum
        beneath a glass dome
a bit like a snow globe
without the snow
        standing
with his long silky
Victorian hair
        and his dead moist nose
and his poignant glass eyes
that keep the sweet mystery
        in their light –
the reflected light
of the deserted gallery
        except for someone
down at the far end
saying
        fur fuck's sake man
come an see this

on a purple velvet rostrum
adorned with
        purple lumps and tassels
a squint silver inscription
I have to stoop
        to decipher
telling of the 100 First prizes
he won
        and the 30 Seconds
with the dignity
of his useful life
        shining bright
in the sealed forgotten air

and maybe they'll clone him
and he'll get to sniff it all over again
           and maybe
they'll stuff me as well –
clone me so I can come back
           and rant and scratch
the same cool black words
all over again
           fur fuck's sake man
come an hear this

A Scottish Talking Poet!
Just press
           the button
and off he goes

The Poetry Reaper

sitting in The Scotia
after John McGarrigle who-
was-killed-in-The Clutha's funeral,
wolfing
triangular tuna sandwiches
and listening to someone singing
We Shall Overcome
into a feedback microphone, I ask
Bobby Christie
if he remembers walking home
twenty-five years ago
from Tom Leonard's Writers' Group
in Paisley in the dark
with
towering orange streetlamps
and turning left into Penilee Road
where a cop in a panda
wound down his window and asked us
what we had in our bags
to which we shouted *POETRY!*
in unison,
lifted
thick majestic photocopies
and *Poems of Thirty Years*
by Edwin Morgan into the air
as he looked on in horror
and told us to be on our way
and not to do it again

and Bobby
disappeared over the hill
as I turned right into Atholl Crescent
to go to a house where I no longer live
to talk to people who
are no longer there,
and Jim Ferguson
is wearing a burning red tie
and brandishing a virtual cigarette, and
We Shall Overcome was sung
by Joan Baez in 1963, it's really
hard to believe, it feels
as if yesterday
has still to happen, tomorrow
is already gone

Charles the Third

On the day the Queen became
Britain's longest EVER EVER serving monarch
in the history of humankind
and all who sail in her
a male presenter
on the BBC's Number 1 Channel
introduced a waving woman who may
have been
the Queen
or may only have been someone who
makes their living pretending to be
the Queen
which made me leap to my feet
and scream at my wife
Jesus Christ, it's dead poet Charles Bukowski
dressed up as the Queen
or a Queen lookalike!
He must have manufactured his fatal death
and forged a new identity for himself
as the longest serving British monarch!
I ran
and grabbed
a tome published by Black Sparrow Press
to prove my conclusion
and there he was
in a black and white photo
near the end of the book
behaving exactly like the Queen
with that ugly lovely Grand Canyoned face
and a crinkled twinkle in his wankered eye
that says
Come and have a few beers with me baby
and then we'll fuck our brains out
and live together in squalor and death
and I'll probably write a book of poems

about it, you won't know
what's hit you
or reciting the first line of
my favourite poem called
something for the touts, the nuns,
the grocery clerks and you ... which is
One has everything and One has nothing
if it was the Queen who was saying it
which it isn't,
and my wife,
or someone who looks like my wife,
was completely gobsmacked and said
Fuck's sake, it really is Charles Bukowski!
How could I ever have doubted you!
and we all lived
happily ever after
except the real Queen who's out there
buried alive in Bukowski's coffin

The Great Glasgow Science Tower Disaster

It rotates! It rotates! It rotates!
or at least it's meant to
when it's working
which
isn't very often, in fact
it's been permanently temporarily
out of order for years
as it stands alone at the edge of the Clyde
looking all space-agey
with its swivelly cameras and silver ladders
and its bird-skulled capsule at the top
with outstanding views of Glasgow.
and there's a landline ringing somewhere
all the time,
a man
whose job appears to be
probing out clots of gunk
from between the pink steps
including feathers, leaves, straws, plastic
forks.
and the whole thing resembles
an abandoned sacrificial altar on Mars
discovered by some rickety wheeled robot,
or a beacon for unwary space travellers
with a repeating message that says
Dear unwary space traveller
Do not come here at all costs, but if you do
then on no account use the lift in this tower
because the cable will snap
and you'll go
plunging fast as fuck,
and your only chance of survival will be
to jump in the air in the split second
just before the lift hits the ground
which is theoretically impossible
It rotates! It rotates! It rotates!

Kylie's Pants are Calling Me

An exhibition of Kylie Minogue's stage clothes was held in Glasgow's Kelvingrove Museum in 2007

Kylie's pants are calling me,
Kylie's
      gold
            hot
                  pants
that she wore in the video for 'Spinning Around'
are calling me
from their subterranean chamber
next to the carrot cake emporium,
                  the shop selling
exquisite Vettriano fridge magnets,
                            stretchy green lizards,
World War One colouring posters
    (mainly brown and red)

Kylie's primeval arse

is telling me to press my nose against
the fully alarmed glass case,
                  sniff the air,
then sprint upstairs where
people are pouring in to point
at a fibre glass Elvis with a halo in white,
curl, pot belly, feeble crotch
                            a man
begins to thump some Beethoven
                  on his one o'clock organ,
makes me think of *A Clockwork Orange*
(the rammy in the theatre,
quite near the start)

It's a clichéd river of Glaswegian humanity!

fighting their way through to look at
a vertical row of severed birds' heads
with the smallest at the bottom –
a sparrow (nailed in place),
a finch (upside down),
a kingfisher,
an eagle,
a big duck,
something I don't know
and a curlew
all looking honoured to be here
in the general vicinity
of tiny children in orange jackets
holding hands
and screaming in delight at a velociraptor
                              programmed to growl
                              every thirty seconds
on a false, Jurassic, carpet
of grass

heads and arses,
the stuff of life

Kylie's pants are calling me,
but I must resist
and go to inspect Darwin's tray of beetles,
a young mum saying to her two little boys
Do you know what the head of a skeleton is called?
It's called A SKULL!,
                        an autistic boy jumping
on the spot
and flapping his arms,
loving every wonder to come,
an angry harpy clutching her right breast,
feathers sprouting
from her neck,
a boy in a wheelchair picking his nose
as he gazes up at the spitfire,

                the gannets,
the starlings turning slowly
in the breeze, which
                    isn't
even there

wings and arses,
the stuff of life

                    sea-
horses and star-
fish

Sir Roger the elephant who got too horny
so they shot him as he chomped his toast,
a small elephant called Kelvin,
an AWOL puffer fish (out on loan),
a photo of a gorilla's hacked-off head
in a bloody bowl of tin,
I must resist!
I must resist!
a lifelike false hand covered in mosquitoes,
stuffed poets,
fossilised gastropods,
people in the café yawning,
mopping up spilt tea,
feeding babies, blowing their brains,
a wee lad laughing at perfect strangers
through a blue plastic lid
as if he'll see it all
                a lot clearer this way

hollow white heads in the air,
every expression known to man

a bible from St. Kilda opened at *Exodus*,
a *Qu'ran* from Kabul, 1879,
a giant photo of Salvador Dali
that seems to be breathing,
    I must resist,
    I must resist,
even though
Miss Minogue's pants are calling me
from their primordial tarpit
next to the shop flogging
artistically challenging Vettriano keyrings,
even though the man with the organ
is now playing the theme tune from *The Sting*

I'm spinnin aroon,
git ooti ma way!

an Antipodean siren
luring me down to my doom

a hive of resident bees,
buttons to hear the cries of extinction,
a selection of eyes to try on for size

a man on a stool, sketching a corpse

flakes of stone, arrowheads, flint,
a beaker vessel from Temple Wood,
birthday balloons, scones and jam,
a selection of
gold,
hot,
pants

Do you know what the head of a skeleton is called?

a tot coming up the entrance steps,
shouting YES! with each one he scales

He's Behind You

Tommy tells me
               he has a book,
The Outsider by Albert Camus,
signed by Stanley Baxter
The Queen!

There was nothing
               else in reach.
He had to
live for the moment,
or lose it   for good.

The inky transvestite flourish
                       above
a blurred absurdist paperback shape.
The existential musings of
             a Drumchapel dialect
pantomime dame.

                  I think
of Stanley Baxter in full drag
shooting an Arab on an African beach,
dying cracked in a squashed-up car.

Parliamo Algeria.

Sanoffy

Sanoffy

Sanoffy nice day
fur contumplaytin
thi nature uv existence.

Perhaps   out there
there's a copy of *Nausea*
signed by Frankie Howerd,
a copy of *Beyond Good and Evil*
signed by Kenneth Williams,
a copy of *Being and Time*
signed by Sid James.

A copy of *The Rebel* by Albert Camus
      closed on Tony Hancock's bed.

Nearly an armful of comedy blood, and death
disguised as a horse's arse.

Beautiful

this couple have a dog
a sort of dog off the leash
with a small laughing son
and it's
biting the swan on the wing
in the park pond
biting and tearing at
its wing
with the white wing flapping
and the dog snarling
and the couple calling
TOBY TOBY
STOP IT TOBY,
but not
caring
and looking at me
looking at them
and knowing
they've been seen
but not giving a flying fuck
if a beautiful life dies,
and their laughing son
laughing and not giving
a beautiful fuck if
the swan lives or dies

The Three Junkies

three junkies
huv jist gone up that road pal
three junkies
huv jist passed me
wan aftur thi other
az ah stood here in thi rain
an they wur aw
lookin at ma bike
ma thousan poun bike
each wan
wuz
slowin doon
an eyein up
ma thousan poun bike
fur fuck sake
wan hud a ginger bottle
in iz haun
az e slowed doon
ah cud see it in iz eyes
oan a Saturday afternoon
three junkies
huv jist gone up that road pal
so jist watch yersel
an huv a good day
an if another junkie
so much as looks at me
ahll kill thi fuckin cunt

The Three Dancers

kissed
by air-conditioned
currents

a dandelion clock
and
two
clots
of fluff

are performing
a small ballet

softly
twirling around
each
other

on
the shining tiles
in HMV

**a man
made of
paracetamol**

Big Bang

The door of the bus is going BANG!
with a huge BANG!
as it opens
to let people on or off, but not
every time
to keep us guessing, and making
wee girls pushing their prams
into the space for prams
and wee old men
with their hurricane headline tabloids
have a heart attack as it goes BANG!, the outside
trying to get in,
and girls without prams
saying *Whit wiz that big bangin sound?*
because it's so loud and sudden
that nobody believes it could
just be a door
opening and closing and going BANG!, the inside
trying to get out, it sounds
more like
a bomb,
or a T-Rex
ramming the side of the world we're riding,
as a wee woman says to her own reflection
Ah nearly shat masel
its fuckin ridickyaluss ti huv
a door makin a noise like that
kin they no git it fixt fur fuck sake
ah nearly shat masel as the door goes BANG!

The Moons of Uranus

the usual route past the swings
while desperately trying to remember
the name of the biggest moon of Uranus
as this old man
is calling his out-of-control dog
called Ruby, he's calling
         Ruby   *Ruby*
in a rhythmic way
without a hint of panic
with one of these ball-slinging gizmos
in his hand

and I'm sure
the biggest moon of Uranus is Titania
but it might be Triton or Titan
although I think they belong
to Neptune and Saturn, I'm
nearly sure it's Titania
and why are so many moons
named after fairies like Puck
or real people from *The Tempest*
such as
Caliban and Miranda

and I'm convinced
someone told me
that Saturn is so light it would
float on water, it would
float in your bathtub alongside
your rubber duck,
and there are so many moons out there
orbiting so many planets spinning round
so many suns with all their
hard coalesced material forming coherent shapes
that one of them somewhere

has got to be called
Ruby
as I circle towards the gates
and the man is still calling
         Ruby   *Ruby*
in a Zen Buddhist way,
and he's calling so much and looking
in my direction I'm beginning to think
that maybe it's me he's calling
even though it's never been my name

Young Disciples

a man of fifty or less,
waiting for the green man
while wearing a lilac satiny sport top
and white shorts
down to his knees
and yellow rubbery sport shoes
beside
a single slice of tomato
slipped from a sandwich
on the pavement
with strange symbols carved
into his hair like something from Peru
you can only see
from the sky, is yelping
meaningful incomprehensibilities
to anyone who'll listen,
and making wavy undulating moves
with his arms
while two boys
stand right behind him laughing their heads off
and making wavy undulating moves
with their arms

Unclean

a manky white van
outside
the church

the words
WASH ME

fingered in
its dirt

The Lanes

there are druggings and couplings
and a wretched trembling of knees
in these quaintly narrow Glasgow lanes,
it's a tradition!,
penetration, violence, desperate liaisons
among perpetrators of all sexes,
and territorial pishings against the stone
or in natural animal semen doorways
with loud alcohol spewing,
and passionate kickings,
and mechanical prickings at dark time
in these alleys that worm between our places,
and lots
of aesthetically orgasmic
civilised coital architecture
above their heads, the moon

blood   tears
spunk   stars

but in the daysun it's not too bad at all,
quite nice,
with stubbled cooks
swallowing sneaky relaxing smoke
in their splashed jackets and cookery hats
next to slop skips,
and people taking short cuts
from one shoppers' paradise to another,
which they wouldn't dream of doing
when night falls,
oh no,
because then they'll have their throats slit
or get spirited away to live in the sex trade,
it's a tradition!

The Postman

as I stare up at the face
of a mythical man in pain
staring straight down from a wall
a postman in red coming out of a café
tells me if
I walk down the hill and turn right
into Waterloo Street
there's the most beautiful building
in Glasgow
about twenty yards along
with a FOR SALE sign on it
and clustered people smoking
at the foot of the steps
beneath two jaunty
turbany-kilty-Robin-Hood-type figures
who seem to be ready to start dancing
any moment now,
and there are six small smiling heads,
and at the very top,
if you shield your eyes from the sun,
there are bits sticking straight out which look
like elephant trunks,
and it's a real shame
what they've allowed to happen
to the building,
and when I go and look
he's absolutely correct

Freaks

Someone is whistling *Dance of the Cuckoos,*
also known as the Laurel and Hardy theme,
as they pass the blue plaque
on the sooty wall of the covered alley
on Trongate
which says
Stan Laurel performed here,
which could
confuse some people
as to why he would perform in an alley,
not realising that it truly means
the Panopticon Music Hall
which rises above our heads
in courageous Italianate wedding cake
flaky-paint-layers of bold arched windows
and mysterious Colosseum numerals
where Tom Thumb
and Solomon the Man Monkey
and Cary Grant in lipstick
probably trod the boards
in the full glare of humanity,
with all of it
balanced outrageously upon
the baby boutique shop,
and the sweetie shop selling
Edinburgh Rock and *Old Fart Fudge,*
and the bleeping amusement arcade
with a small woman sitting with
her legs dangling
next to a giant red waste bin
and sucking enthusiastically on a tall fag

Hatrack Monsters

there's a subliminal difference
                      in the expressions
of the two dragon/demon/alien/lion
                            hybrid nightmare faces
     on the sculpted heads
erupting out of
     the spectacular lean sandstone
of James Salmon's masterpiece
               on St. Vincent Street,
with the left one,
         precisely above the steps
leading up to
     the recruitment office,
seeming to let rip
         with a contented yawn,
while the right one,
         who's significantly lower down
a few feet away,
         is roaring or puking or getting ready
to take someone's flesh off
               precisely above
the doorway
     leading into
the healthy option salad restaurant,
                         and maybe
the left one is a bit older than the right,
           and has put his killing teeth away,
and cherishes the quiet life

The Details

I'll know when I see it

a secret
hiding at the edge of the details,
                                  overlooked,
a suggestion of a feeling that says
Here is what it's all about,
Here is what we're left with

serpents coiling out of stone,
classical maidens with glorious breasts,
a woman with wings playing two flutes
at the same time,
fruit, fronds, symbols of abundance
on the affluent walls of mansions and halls,
The Baltic Chambers,
The Lion Chambers,
a man crouching behind a net
to stop things getting in, things getting out,
                                    a secret
skulking at the margins of the mind

the ubiquitous prows of ships
slicing through trade winds,
the merchants and moguls and magnates,
a naked child with its face erased
astride a seahorse,
I'll know when I see it, the key,
the shapes that we believe we should take,
the grumpy face of an Argonaut beast,
Neptune dripping fish from his curls,
                                    gills and goddesses,

scrolls, swirls, expressionless men
supporting the great weights
of banks converted into boutiques

columns and tridents
and urns that belong in a cemetery,
bellows of brutal wealth and prosperity,
Dickensian men called Baird and Donaldson
glowering down, the names
        AYR and PAISLEY
above a casino,
entwined initials, coats of arms,
the instruction LET   GLASGOW   FLOURISH,
it's all in the details of time and space,
it's all in what isn't there anymore,
the promises JUSTICE   WISDOM   CONTENTMENT,
the fading traces of obliterated INSURANCE
and WHOLE and THE something
                      or other,
        still visible
where they used to be

a paint-caked pair of trousers
                draped over a ledge,
an imagined silent face
at the attic window
of an unhappy warehouse

Here is what it's all about,
Here is what we're left with,
the secret waiting to be found,
                      layers
of what is gone and what is waiting to go,
empires that rose, waiting to fall

International Brigade Statue on Custom House Quay

never been down
        these steps
                before,
and *La Pasionaria*
      on her black steel column,
    facing the fence,
edging the river,
        is looking particularly attractive
          with her stylish housemoth-brown dress
              flaring out behind her,
  and her determined civil war stance,
  and her eyes seeking something in the sky,
and her unsurrendered fibre glass arms
        with clenched fists
               stretching up
    as if she's about to fly,
a Spanish superwoman.
              and the truth first told by Zapata
      better to die on your feet than live forever
  on your knees
is below her feet,
      a man is leaning against a wall spooning yoghurt,
          a man is sprawled asleep on the grass,
    turns onto his side for maximum comfort,
        a man is tenderly balancing
              his bald baby on his knee, the Clyde
is breathing, the lifebelt
    is in its proper place,
              it's what
    they would have died
to save.

The Muppet Show

Glasgow, 13/7/2018

FUCK OFF
YOU TINY-HANDED
ORANGE-FACED CUNT
painted
in red
on card
is one of the less ambiguous messages
at the Death to Donald Trump rally
in George Square in the sunshine
as is
BAWBAG
TRUMP'S A FUD
RAGE AGAINST THE TANGERINE
TRUMP'S AN EEJIT
said in a bubble by a stuck-on cat
a pussy on a placard

a Saltire saying FUCK OFF YA FANNY
a Welsh dragon saying I HATE FASCISTS

as
babies dreaming in prams
and not in cages
obliviously mix with ministers
political or religious
activists and re-activists
urologists
sociologists
anarchists
telephonists
taps aff sunburnt bampots
dogs with signs
saying PUGS AGAINST DESPOTS

toddlers with signs
saying TODDLERS AGAINST TRUMP
old ladies booing when prompted
cannabis smokers
energy drinkers
muslims and atheists
and candlestick makers
FUCK OFF YA RACIST CUNT
DONALD WHERE'S YER CONSCIENCE

a Buddhist monk who's had enough
holding a sign that says
TRUMP'S A MUPPET

two orange balloons
in a transparent bag
which looks like a big orange arse
with a blond wig
as American tourists pass by
on the open-top sight-seeing bus
taking pictures and saying
Oh Elmer, isn't this quaint!

Techno Tin Bin Man

outside St. Enoch subway
a techno tin bin man
is sitting with his
yellow hard hat
glasses
an old smile on his face
as he batters
and clatters
his dustbin drum kit
with lids for cymbals
and two
automaton ginger cats
gyrating
on silver buckets
with a sign that says
do not feed the cats

another man
in psychedelic leggings
with letters carved
into his head
is performing
a disturbingly rhythmic
time-warp-mime-dance
to rave music
thumping out of
an unseen speaker
which is sublimely hideous
and everyone is
laughing and dancing
and having a great time

Flaw of Nature

above the trees   drifting
soothingly along the wide sky
is a cloud in the guise
of a West Highland Terrier
with its four legs clearly
in the act of running
and its tail erect with
neck,
head,
tongue,
and just the ears missing
to perfect the illusion   which

is conceivably chasing
the mouth-sized green ball   which

has rolled,
logically, onto
the frozen pond at my feet
and slowed to a stop halfway across
leaving
a curving, ethereal,
obedient trail   and
a crystal-sharp
planet-shaped reflection of itself
on the ice

Unfathomable

human remains
        in separate puddles

a little blue paintbrush
                            not much thicker
                      than the channels
        on my palms,
acrylic,
bought in WH SMITH,
                petrified bristles
        unsoftened
by the rains

uncharted water

a flipper of black plastic
                that used to be half
of something else

I think
a bin lid

rhythmically
        drifting
                like
                            Mary Celeste
on an ocean above
        a double-yel-
low line

Marcelitis and Other Diseases

I'm not too keen on mime artists.
There's absolutely no need
for mime artists with their ropes and glass
and walls that aren't there,
and exaggerated facial expressions
and dodgy facial make-up, Christ,
they make me puke, there's nothing
funny about them,
and nothing that says that
this is a valuable contribution to
the overall artistic heritage of mankind
with their rope and glass
and walls that aren't there and doing things
that aren't the least bit funny,
they make me VOMIT, and don't get me started
on Marcel Marceau, the only thing that's worse
than a mime artist is a French mime artist,
we were given voices
so we could say words,
so we could use language to express ideas, ideology,
if God had wanted us to be mime artists
he wouldn't have given us voices

free speech,
that's what it's all about

and there's nothing clever
about pandas
either,
they just sit there in their fat fur doing nothing
and can't even make little pandas
without some help from a syringe,
the male is totally useless,
an arsehole!
they should just be allowed

to be extinct, die out, the last one
in a glass case in a museum, there's nothing
worse than a panda, in fact
the only thing that's worse than a panda
is a mime artist, or a mime artist
in a panda suit,
the whole lot of them with their make-up and top hats
and figure-hugging leotards, they should all
be made to suffer in silence, aye,
let's see them miming pain when they're hanging
from the gallows or gasping in the chamber,
aye, let's see them do that!

Daily Planet

a man who's been
on this planet a long time
with glasses
blue anorak
beige baseball cap
and grasping a thin white bag that says
THANK YOU
HAVE A NICE DAY

is staring
with simmering disgust

at a man who's not been
on this planet a long time
sitting two seats away
on the bus
with white stockings
cheapo French maid outfit
purple flowing wig
and a cautiously happy smile on his face

A Fly

We've adopted a fly.
He flew in 5 days ago and hasn't gone out again.

We didn't kill him with paper or fist.
We call him Vincent
because Vincent Price was the star
of the first version of *The Fly* released in 1958.

We've learned not to hate.
He goes from room to room
to see what we have.
He sits on the wall of the bathroom
as I look at myself in the mirror.
He sits on the wall of the kitchen as I boil a kettle.
He sits on the screen of the TV
as we watch *University Challenge*
and rubs his legs with glee.

Your starter for 10 –
How long does a fly live? What does a fly see?
What does a fly think?

Does a fly know the capital
of Burkina Faso?

He's a tiddler of a piddler.
He plays with bacteria and filth.
We've shown him the open window
but he doesn't want to go.
He wants to stay with us
and look after us until we have to die.

Either that or die himself
in a couple of weeks.

We'll bury him in a matchbox
down by the whirlies,
entrust him to the care of baby Jesus.

Your starter for 10 –
How long does a human live? What does a human see?
What does a human think?

He's the son we never wanted.
If he could speak he'd probably say *Help Me! Help Me!*
in a high-pitched voice.

*The capital of Burkina Faso
is Ouagadougou!*

Bowel Screening Test

I'm over 50
and I'm ready
to test my bowel

I pull a book from the bookshelf
I don't look at the title
I put it in the toilet bowl
and cover it with luxury toilet roll

I do half a keech, stop, slap a little lump
into the space provided

close the tab, write the date,
complete the keech, dispose of the stick

The book is
A Disaffection by James Kelman

There are diagrams on the instruction leaflet
but none of them shows a book being used

This is my own invention
It has to be the correct size to fit neatly
into the bowl, create a secure platform
It needs to feel right

The second sample is
Treasure Island by Robert Louis Stevenson,
the third sample is
Lolita by Vladimir Nabokov

It's totally random
I do it by touch
It has to be hardback to take the strain

I wash my hands

There is no hidden meaning

All I do now is wait

A Clockwork Nokia

I love my NOKIA from 2004
I love the way it fits completely into my hand

I love the fact that
the letters and numbers
have all been rubbed away over the years
and are no longer there

The clusters are all gone
I do it by memory
I do it without thinking

If I stop to think I get it wrong
The alphabet
explodes in my head

I've saved the best messages from
the years of my life
especially the one from my wife that says
'Great stuff my man. Get home here
and stick your penis in my vagina.'
also
'Gin!'
'death.'
'I ate a pack of twiglets.'
'Ya lazy bastard! Get that tea on.'
also
'juicy'
'Tongues?'
'Pasta on! Knickers off!'

I once sent the message
'Ah Luv Yew.' to my wife
but sent it to Alan McCready by mistake
He was deeply touched, but understood

I have no camera or contacts
I insist in using correct punctuation
Apostrophes and capital letters
No shortcuts or symbols

Someday my memory will be used up
and I won't be able to hear anyone anymore
My limits will be done

I am a dispensable member of society
I need to be euthanised for crimes against normality

'umma gumma,
 show's yur bumma.'

Reptile House

there's a cage on top of the cooker
in the kitchen
of the house where I used to live
a cat   a guinea pig
a mouse
cower to one side   on the other
   a miniature python
      a miniature boa constrictor
slither around in the straw
I say
you can't keep them
all together in the same cage
mum says   it'll be okay

the jaw of the python begins to stretch
as it takes the cat's head
into its mouth   the curtains
are closed
in the corner of the living room
behind the sofa
a normal-sized python methodically
swallows a man alive   he's shrivelled
dark skinned   doesn't make
a sound   slowly
disappears from sight

Reptilius Completelymentalus

Giggling in bed continuously
with sheets and pillows
and closed curtains to keep out
the daylight,
reciting
favourite lines
from Hammer Film *The Reptile*
we watched last night
for the third time this week
such as
There's nothing to see   only to hear
and *Waiting   ah waiting   aren't we all,*
or banging
invisible voodoo drums
like the ones in *The Plague of the Zombies,*
or best of all
reciting killer lines
from *Dracula Prince of Darkness*
such as
There'll be no morning for us
and *Rum-ti-tiddly-tum-ti-tum*
instead of doing
important things like
memorising a poem or painting a painting
or going for a bracing walk
to a mountain or a fountain or a railway station
or hopping a thousand miles faster than anyone
has ever hopped a thousand miles
appears
to make
more sense to me
and is less harmful than morphine, Maltesers,
searching the daily newspapers
for whatever's there
behind the dark – you see

the illusion of horror can be a comfort,
reptiles and devils can be your friends,
can give you something fine to hold on to
as the days and the decades hurry past,
faceless men wearing papier mâché masks
while saying
things like
Do you believe in life after death Miss Forbes?
can make it all feel worthwhile

Unexpect the Expected

a red message flashes
                      frustratingly
                               frequently
    on the right of the screen
saying
If you die unexpectedly...
as I'm busy deleting important emails at random,
                which is obviously trying to tell me
something essential about
                        insurance, death,
providing adequate comfort
 for the loved ones I leave behind
if I die unexpectedly,
      as opposed
                to expectedly
which people expect to happen
            when you're lying in a hospital bed
or a care home or an oxygen tent
                    at the age of ninety-nine
with everyone
      sitting around staring into your face,
    saying *he's had a good innings*
                    and expecting you to croak
as they listen to the wind
             whispering
on the other side of
the skin,
            and it would be so nice
if I could send out invitations
             well in advance to those concerned
      saying

please come round at two minutes past three
                      this afternoon as I'm expecting to
     deconstruct into
nothingness ...
                                       synchronise your watches,
       latecomers will not
be admitted

The Pedestrian Crossing Light Bulb Changer

The Pedestrian Crossing Light Bulb Changer
                        is in the act
of changing the light bulb
at the pedestrian crossing
                        that spans the gap
between the chip shop
    and the funeral parlour,
he's
wearing
    a radioactive-wasp-yellow jacket,
he's
pulling
out the old and
slipping in the new, he's
keeping the WAIT in our lives
                        buzzing bright, showing us
the way to go on our happy journeys
towards death, it
                never
occurred to me that
somebody actually has to go round
changing the light bulbs
on the Pedestrian Crossings, as if
it's a naturally regenerating phenomena, as if
                        they know instinctively when
they're dying, like mayflies, or elephants
or men

The Lights

at the funeral Mass

between the ringing
of a bell
and the beating
of a gong

a blissful baby boy
is

scraping his toy ambulance
along the wooden pew,
cleaning the bench
with his blue hat

and looking
in

the opposite direction
to everybody else
at something above,
beyond, our heads

Earth on Heaven

a smiling white cherub
playing a violin

hanging
by
a silver cord

from
a back court fence

above
the jobbies and straws

a piece of
broken plastic wing

ACH FUCK IT
stencilled on a wall

All Yesterday's Parties

at the
same time as

a deflated
maroon balloon
with the number 21
sparkling on its skin

is waltzing
from one side of the

street to the

other

a man walks past me
singing *Mellow Yellow*

**a man
made of
wine**

Whatever You Do Don't Smile

looking subnormal in a photo booth
only takes a neutron of the consciousness
it took
in the old days
when you had to wait a week
for 4 sloppy photos
to slide out of the slot
in a strangely sexual way
on the side of a weird machine
with a wee overworked man inside
frantically developing at the speed of light,
while now
you twirl the chair to the demanded height
and listen to the female robot instructions
and place your digital head
precisely
within the red oval
and *whatever you do don't smile*
whatever you do don't smile,
until it's all done
and you get your pictures 51 seconds later
and stare at them in disbelief
and do it all again
in the hope that this time
Brad Pitt's or The Elephant Man's
or anyone else's face will be there
instead of your own

Parking Meter

dad took me to see *Jaws* in Glasgow in 1975

we had to stand in a queue which went along
the street
then round the corner and up
a hill

we were near the end, but didn't lose hope

it took so long until it started to move
snailing down the hill then round the corner,
we found the last two seats
seven eighth's of the way back

right at the edge,
close to EXIT

later
dad had to go out and drop
more money in the meter

I kept looking to my left, wondering when
he'd reappear

he was away for ages, slipped back into his space
just in time to see the fisherman's head
come out from the hole in the hull of his boat

under the water,
people screaming then laughing because
they had just been screaming

we wanted to scream,
it was great

we are alive

later
Robert Shaw being crunched by a pneumatic shark
costume blood spurting out of his mouth

he died in real life in 1978 and dad died in 1976

Memento Mori

on the bus
wondering
why it is
whenever I look down
at the blank white expanse
of the bathroom sink
or my hands within
the cold running water
or the toothpaste spittle
swirling away
I always get a bright flash
in my head
of a photograph of dad
wearing his grey-white anorak
and with his arms outstretched
and pretending to sing an old song
called 'Harbour Lights'
as the day is getting dark
beneath a sign above the door
of a B & B in Weymouth
which says
Welcome to Harbour Lights
and which he must have
picked especially
because of its name, a song
he liked,
or maybe
he really is singing,
I was upstairs in a room at the time
and only remember the photograph,
not the life, and
the driver's face
is reflected in his mirror, and
my face is reflected
in the back of a seat

Tom Leonard's Funeral

Clydebank, 12/1/2019

as we cross the Erskine Bridge
the taxi driver says he thinks
humanist funerals are best

you can choose your own music
and people can tell
little antidotes

we read a recipe
for lentil soup

as the phones are turned off
and silence
descends
an order of service
with Tom's smile on it
falls from the balcony
and hits a woman in the stalls
on the head

a child laughs
a ringtone sounds

someone swears
it's only human

the curtain is closed

The Cockett Cats

St. Peter's Church, Cockett, Swansea

The Cockett cats,
fatted on tinned mush, market mince,
wild Welsh mice
they happen to rip – slip, cattishly,
through skews in the fencing,
congregate
in the busy silent graveyard, slink
the way they're built to slink
among the massed brambles,
swaying grasses – park
themselves
irreverently
on top of glassy modern
or made-to-measure Victorian stones
with names like
Theophilus, Benjamin,
Cordelia and Claude – to get
a better look at each other
doing what they do –
looking at each other –
random particles forming a whole, icicles
that cling to circles, winter, ignore

unless completely necessary,
the slow coated humans
who walk
with milk containers full of water,
                the labels unpeeled,
to put down flowers,
                the costs unpeeled,
talk to the soil,
scrub on the surfaces,
slosh away spiders, slugs or leaves

from the gold-worded marble pots,
the rolled away silver lids,
headless cherubs,
archetype angels – articles
of genuine faith, cold spikes
that grow on the residues
of the old aged, young aged, the murdered,
the drowned in a Gower holiday bay,
the natural causes, the lost loved, stay well
out of their way until
they've all vanished home

The Projector's Broken and is Never Going to be Fixed

Travelled to see *Star Trek Into Darkness*
with Benedict Cumberbatch at 11 a.m.
and there was no one there
to tear my ticket,
                and when
I walked inside
it was so dark I couldn't find a seat
until my eyes began to accept
that this is the way it's supposed to be.
                                    I could
make out a handful of souls
sitting towards the back,
and then the sound of the adverts
came crashing on
but the screen was still blank
and the sound went off as well
and we were
left
in transcendental blackness
                            in unedited silence
until a woman came in with a torch
and said
*the projector's broken
and is never going to be fixed.*
                              On the way
home on the 7 bus
the glass was so filthy
I couldn't tell if the shapes
on the other side
were humans or cars or traffic lights,
and it occurred to me

that maybe I've recently kicked the bucket
and the grim little cinema is some sort
of preposterous waiting room
and maybe
the realm of the living
is exactly the same as the realm
of the dead.

Beat Poem

Heart's gone haywire,
                      it's going
BEAT
BEAT
BEAT

BEAT
BEAT
BEAT

a rogue pause, invisible pulse,
it's me
at half past three
lying on a National Health table
the colour of black
with my shirt off
and my socks
rolled down to the   ANKLES
and my pants
pulled down to the   KNEES,
                      or was it
just the socks?
It happened so fast
there was no time
to have
lethal electrodes glued to my ribs,
sparky metal
clipped to my   TESTICLES,
                      or was it
just the ribs it happened
too fast there was no
        TIME
to anoint my hands
with dispensable spurts, the sterile nurse
the colour of green

says she's glad
I don't have a hairy chest
with its unnecessary nipples
no use for suckling   BABIES, the wires
linked to some sickly machine, my life
being darkly scratched
like an earthquake
on a cheapo feed of paper, every BEAT,
every sweet inexplicable BEAT
separating me from   ETERNITY,
which is a line they used in *Fantastic Voyage*
starring Raquel Welch
who my nurse looks nothing like

Jimmy Johnstone

Jimmy Johnstone
               in Uddingston.

       A garden amongst the semi-detached
clippered hedges, numbered bins.
A throw in from
         the slow food shop,
open *Morning*
              Noon and
                       Night.

Wee Man statue. Strip of bronze.
               Sleeves rolled up, socks rolled down.
        Punching the sky. A football Earth
            beneath his boot, round and round,
      year after year, dribbling for peanuts.
League. Cup. Kick. Goal.
The same, then
             the same,
                     again.
Everything, nothing.
Humanly perfect.
        Sculpted from something
older than sense.
The right to be pointless. Poet assassin.
        Ginger predator. 5 foot 2.
A god of flesh
at 3 p.m.

Benches to watch him.
                 Standing stones.
Little floodlights
for evening worship.
Dreggy litter, 12 inch pizza boxes
Freshly Prepared For You.

Stamped-on cans of lager and beer.
A china plate on top of some slugs,
         dishwasher safe,

     a 7
on his shorts.

It's not his face. His hair's too old.
He looks like a tribune from ancient Rome.

                      Jinky is dead.
              Paradise dust.
         Here are today's
league results.
         Here are today's
cup results.

As I leave I gather the junk age crap,
                spill some *Tennent's*
onto my shoe.

Davie Cooper

through the retail park car park
and between the trees
                next to *KFC*
and here's
Rangers winger Davie Cooper
who died of a brain haemorrhage
in 1995
on a brick plinth
with his head too big for his body
and a cobweb spinning from
his left ear

poised
                professionally
focusing
                gracefully
along the path
parallel to the white lines
and the netless goalposts
stretching towards Hamilton Mausoleum
with a sculpted ball
at his left foot

there's a *McFlurry* carton on a penalty spot
a croaking crow on a black fence

a woman is dragging
her dog
                joggers
                            far off
are running round the edge of grass
and stopping and walking

until a trainer blows a whistle
then blows it again
to let them know
         it's okay
                  to breathe

there's an extinct bee on the plinth
an insistent drone from the motorway

Davie's preparing
to belt a free kick
into the postage stamp corner
or flick a pinpoint pass
or swing a mathematical cross
onto the heads of the shadows
of dead Scottish legends
or into the unused dimensions reserved
for legends
yet to be made

the legends pile up

there's plenty of room

Cathkin Park

Municipal oval.
Land of Third Lanark.

Put to sleep in '67.

An Asian man in a long brown shirt
walks the touchline impressively fast.
Round, again, and not slowing down,
never wavering, staying cool.

He churns up phlegm,
but never spits, at least not when
someone
will see.

Perhaps it would be a sacrilege.
This used to be a pitch of faith.

Red crush barriers still in place,
holding back the restless air.

The ghosts are segregated, it seems.
A tree copse, then a sweep of terrace,
a slap of trees, a gap, a slap.
A strange arrangement
on three of the sides.
The fourth is space, except
for a Council worker trying
to start a machine.

A bench with a pair of spray paint names.

*This was us, and now
we're gone.*

All that's left.

Last week's papers, cube shot tubs,
bottles for bingeing, weedstems, moss.
Hooch, voddie, *Tennent's*, of course.
The steps between
the sad proud sections
sucking us down to a crumbled wall
where kids with rattles used to cheer
their brylcreemed heroes, a manky glove,
a single leaf fused onto the wool.

Empty packets of glow sticks, rings.

Lost Age uses for ancient sites.

Inside the copses
are vipers of rubber
skinned from stolen copper cable.
Soggy fleeces from victims unknown.
A graveyard of ritual *Buckfast* glass.

Soft green mounds
like sacred barrows.

Perhaps the mingled players' remains.
Cremated corpses
of managers past.

The turbanned man was here
when I came. He's still pacing off
when I need to leave. Perhaps
he's taking a step for each soul. Perhaps
he's here till the end

of our time.

The hems of his jimjams
starred with mud.
White lines stretching on lumpy grass.

There Was Once a Moment When None of This Existed

There was once a moment before
Jim Baxter played keepie up
at Wembley in black and white, and then it was there
and then it was gone,
there was once a moment before
Tommy Gemmell booted
Helmut Haller up the arse
prior to being sent off in 1969, and then it was there
and then it was gone,
there was once a moment before
Joe Jordan came flying in
to head the ball in 1973,
there was once a moment before
red-haired Billy Bremner
shoved red-haired Jimmy Johnstone
out in a rowing boat at Largs
when they should have been
tucked up in bed,
there was once a moment before
Joe Jordan scored against Yugoslavia in 1974
and Billy Bremner hugged him to death
with a mixture of joy and pride
and sadness and regret, and then it was there
and then it was gone,
there was once a moment before
Kenny Dalglish sent the ball
between Ray Clemence's legs,
there was once a moment before
the Wembley crossbar cracked in two,
there was once a moment before
the ball was given to Archie Gemmill, and then
it was there
and then it was gone,
there was once a moment before
David Narey stuck out his toe,

there was once a moment before
James McFadden hammered the ball from 30 yards,
there was once a moment before
Leigh Griffiths took a free kick
against England after 87 minutes,
there was once a moment before
Leigh Griffiths took another free kick
against England after 90 minutes,
there was once a moment before
Harry Kane equalised three minutes later
which we all knew was going to happen,
there was once a moment before
sometime in the future
when we finally qualified at long last, and then it was there
and then it was gone

Set the Controls For the Heart of The Club Bar in Paisley

Scotland have just beaten Croatia 1–0
in Zagreb
when we least expect it,
and to add to
the amplified wash of unreality
the pub is now playing
back to back songs by Pink Floyd
beginning with
'Set the Controls for the Heart of the Sun'
which I've definitely not heard
in a pub before
with Nick Mason's moody voodoo drums
and Roger Waters' mumbling zombie vocals,
and to enhance even more
the giddy sense of insanity
the barman offers me a choice
of lemon
or lime
to plop in my gin and tonic
which just doesn't happen
in this town.
and Roger has quietly asked
is there anybody in there,
and we're huddling in here like apes feeling
uncomfortably dumb
and wondering if
we imagined it all or someone put something
psychedelic in our drinks
as Roger philosophically winds things up
with
all that is gone   all that's to come ...
which is probably
a 0–0 draw with San Marino.

Empty Fairground

The Twister isn't twisting,
The Terminator isn't terminating,
The Drop Zone isn't dropping, there's not
a soul around
at the magical carnival
beside the Clyde at 9 a.m.
with all the goldfish dead in their bags

the blue kiddies' paddling pool
full of twinkling ring-pulls
and twinkling twinkles, blown leaves, and each
of the human-sized cradles, cages
waiting to be filled
as long as you reach the required height
with purples and greens
and yellows and reds
and splashes of liquid lightning

like blood,
spit,
lips,
laughter, and

electric cables thicker than constrictors,
a Pacific rim bikini surf-bride
wearing a golden Stetson astride
a sweating *Sunset Boulevard* hunk

a *Party in The Sun* sexfun contraption
resplendent with sexual imagery
of ideal sexual people
having sexual conception
before they're sour sixteen
which swivels and swoops
with all

the burlesque bayonet bulbs
preparing to switch on,
fizz,
connect, when it's dark,
reveal

a smiling-mouth gateway to a next world,
eerie stillness,
smells and screams,
whispering metals yet to be invented,
22nd Century capsules, carriages
and higgledy-piggledy dragon dodgems
attractively menacing,
dreaming, waiting

to turn alive
at the press of a button

from someone
secretly sniggering inside
the shuttered get-your-ticket-here hut, because
No Head-On Collisions! are allowed
in this land of enchantment,
This Is The Place To Be!
if you want to *Keep On Bumping!*
beside the shivering, April Clyde

Inflation

the man who blows up
the inflatable castle
in the park
is on his knees
literally   metaphorically
as he methodically unfolds
the soft plastic turrets and walls
and the sun-yellow smiley keep
for all the children
who are nowhere to be seen
to bounce on,
fall on,
laugh on,
and mutters things like
I don't make any money
out of this yi know
and *Is it goin ti rain tomorrow?*
and *Nobody tells me anythin*
to a silent man
probably standing listening
with a white jumper
a black dog on a short lead
as if he
isn't content with his life,
as if he really believes
there's more to this
than making
lots of people happy

Parallel

the
driver
of
a

slowly
moving bus
is having

a
conversation
through the open door
with

a
dwarf
who is moving quickly along
the pavement on
a pair of crutches

The Toothpaste Cage

The toothpaste cage
is in the medicine cabinet

above the sink
next to the toilet

It protects
the old-fashioned
hand-waggled toothbrush
and the toothpaste with red stripes
in the mass-produced tube

Biological incarceration

There is water in the toilet
There is nothing in the water
There is a spare bar of Palmolive
It's good to have a spare bar of Palmolive
in case of emergencies
Earache Earthquake Volcano

Keep yourself clean   Listen

The toothpaste cage
stops my mouth turning black
My lobes boiling
My sphincter spontaneously combusting
It will stop
all war when the time is right
It will stop
terror people lighting up everyone
in churches and stations

It will stop death
whisking away all of our loved ones
It will stop earwigs
crawling into my ears

Supernatural benediction

There's a fly buzzing beside my brain
There are ointments and buds
Endless things
to ease the pain

It will save the world from the world
with minty squeezings
of new-fashioned gunk

The building blocks of life itself
The bottomless spunk of God

The Cork Jugs

Corks. Cork-shaped. Corks made of cork
placed in jugs made of jug. On the landing
outside our flat door, on top of bookcases
made of wood
jammed with books made
of paper. It's not ours to colonise, but no one
normally comes here. It doesn't matter. Our existence
spilling, delightfully,
out of control. Unheard
echoes. Each cork with a year, a milestone
written in spidery biro. Arachnid ink,
scratching slowly around the edge until it meets
itself. Birthday, anniversary, publication,
Valentine's Day. Any excuse for French bubbles.
No births or funerals.
We sometimes pour them out to remember
what we've done. *Look, here is what we've done.*
Put them back in the wrong order. A scrabble
of life. It's nice to know they're there. *We're here.*
This is where we are. Sixty? A hundred?
When the third jug is full we'll find
a fourth. A beloved, intimate ossuary. Our deaths
measured out with champagne corks.

The Choir Windows of Dunblane Cathedral

phallic rocket splashes of
        modern pagan colours
ascend
     from the wooden seats of the choir
to the dark shadowed height
of the holy roof
with undiluted heathen reds,
                pure blues,
                    theological illogical yellows
and bold, natural, innocently blasphemous
pleasures of ice   snow   sun
fire   the four winds
               and best of all
a sweet cradled moon,
          benign cartoon stars
hanging light years off
              in the archangel sky,
                the relentless discarding
     of worn-out seasons,
          breathtakingly daring,
with kaleidoscopic animals
earth   water and storms
        in the second year of
the First World War

        and William Blake's
                in there somewhere,
if you have the time,
with Adam   Eve
trees   grass   pre and post
               or sub-Raphaelite
    art nouveau beauty,
      it painfully
makes me want
to believe, but not quite, despite

        the undeniable presence
of a well-intentioned idea, forgiving and kind,
              an evidence of
humanity at its best
        untainted by the hand of man,
Jesus Christ, it's something
to see

The Shed Man

there's a man outside
who's come to build a shed,
replace the old shed that's
                        rotted
                            away

but he's not
some philanthropic shed builder
building sheds for the benefit of mankind,
bringing sheds to the masses,
he's doing it for cash in hand
which he'll count menacingly at the end,
ready to crack your knee caps if
                        there's a penny out,
with his brontosaurus lorry
and his wee helper
as they build the shed at the speed of light
with the side bits, the back bit,
the front bit with the door,
the base,
the roof,
and all the things that hold it together
with nails and banging and thumping
and people shouting *Fuck!*
as they hammer their fingers at 10 a.m.
it's over,
in no time

there's a new born shed standing there
where there wasn't one before
which is pretty impressive,
and I'm watching The Shed Man in awe
in the furtive gap between the blinds
hoping he doesn't catch my eye
because

I know what he'll be thinking which is
*I can create a shed, I can provide
shelter and warmth for my family
when the apocalypse comes. What can
you do, poet, what can YOU do?*

Post Office Masks

the local post office is selling stamps
and envelopes and get well cards
and a generous selection of masks
of stupefyingly famous people
including Lady Gaga
and Tony Blair
made of cardboard and elastic
with little holes for you to stare through,
but it would be
much more satisfying
if they sold people from history
no one would recognise any more
such as Marie Curie who discovered STUFF
or Julius Caesar who invented assassination
or Julius Robert Oppenheimer who built The Bomb
or Friedrich Nietzsche who invented stand-up comedy
or Jack the Ripper who invented serial killing
or Jesus who invented Jesus,
and we could all walk around
the up-to-date precincts
basking in a frisson of nostalgia
for happier times
of moral hygiene and genocide,
and end the day with a party where
we all get blitzed and dance around
to 70's glam rock
in Franz Kafka's living room with everyone
holding hands and wearing a Franz Kafka mask
who invented waking up and finding
you've turned into an insect

Toddlers in the Park

too young for school,
too old to be still unborn, sperm,
egg,
slopped from the domain
of dark matter eternity
to find themselves
wobbling on this glorious grass
in this stewing bouncy castle park
with their new arms excitedly outstretched
and formed from dust, us, reaching
for soapy bubbles, reaching
for all of everything
they've still to know, everything
of no importance,
with their yellow floppy sun hats
and unquestioning nursery smiles,
their battery cars and skin balloons, crying
for nipple dummies, laughing
at kites, swimming dogs
with balls in their mouths
and ducks gliding on the oval pond
feathered in essential pointlessness,
and adults
who are way above them
and way below,
too old to be still unborn, sperm,
egg,
yolked with dumb knowledge,
laughing, crying, knowing
nothing and knowing
that's everything they need to know

An Idiot

Instead of reading *The Idiot*
by Dostoyevsky,
which is open at page
                            78
and
                            79
in my right hand,
I'm busy waggling
the all-singing-all-dancing
holographic bookmark
someone gave me
back and forth
in a poetically cretinous style
with my left hand
which features
                            4

elegant skeletons
marching in step
with a necropolis in the background
and a Halloween moon in the sky
and makes
the skeletons appear to actually move
in a committed *I'm-coming-to-*
kill-you-as-soon-as-possible way

Brilliant!

and they seem to be armed
with an axe, a dagger,
a chainsaw from Texas,
and possibly a feather duster
which could be a cleaver,
and if you waggle extremely fast
they look extremely camp
and not
very scary at all

and on the back
there's a souvenir shop sticker
that says
    £3,
and it's
    57
seconds of my life
I'm never going to see again but who cares
It's magic!

Confess

As I searched for the grave
of Thomas De Quincey
in St. Cuthbert's deathyard
in Edinburgh
I nearly stepped on
a foetus-curled corpse
or a corpse-curled foetus
beneath a white blanket
a shroud
on a hard slab
in the shadow of the castle,
unutterable infinity   I could
make out
the curve of the bottom
thighs
feet
the head was shapeless
a big shapeless unhead – he, or she,
could well have been dead
or alive or somewhere in between
with a brace of dry vodka bottles
or maybe just one, a few
drops
of natural water,
rectangular packets
unutterable infinity in   fin   i   ty,
I couldn't
find his stone
among the green-cheeked cherubs
the skulls
the clanging of the trams,
I read each one
except the one
the dead human was dreaming on
and someday   years from now

I'm going to go back
and tell it to stand up
so I can see once and for all if
it's sleeping above
the opium-eaten bones
of Thomas De Quincey
with the doves and the bats
and the pealing of the bells

Chips, Paracetamol and Wine

CHIPS, PARACETAMOL AND WINE
is what I've to get at the supermarket,
but I know I'll forget
unless I keep saying it to myself
like a ritual purification,
CHIPS, PARACETAMOL AND WINE,
because
there are so many beguiling distractions
between here and *Tesco*
such as the fluttery fan
of bloody pigeon feathers
in the middle of the road,
or the grasp of crisp shrivelled flowers
taped to a fence outside the *Burgh Bar*
with RIP TOMMY MURPY
written on the brown paper wrapper,
the missing
H
accelerating the loneliness,
CHIPS, PARACETAMOL AND WINE
CHIPS, PARACETAMOL AND WINE,
or the perfectly flat Pickled Onion *Space Raiders* packet
in a perfectly flat black puddle,
or the teapots and lampshades and suitcases
in the Hospice Charity Shop window
where I'm distracted from my distractions
by my own close-up reflection
swept backwards in the wind,
CHIPS, PARACETAMOL AND WINE
CHIPS, PARACETAMOL AND WINE,
or the awkward shoeshine shadow shuffle of people in black
about to enter, or just departing,
the Kelburne Funeral Home in the mad past noon sunlight,
I'm almost there
almost there,

CHIPS, PARACETAMOL AND WINE
CHIPS, PARACETAMOL AND LIFE,
keep saying it to myself,
saying it to myself,
CHIPS, DEATH AND LIFE.
Made it.

Stop

the bus driver says it's really nice
to see the children in the park
it's been such
a wet winter
and it'll do them good to get some real
fresh air, he points out
he's wearing shades
but he's not vain it's only because
of all the dust it's too much
and his skin gets flaky, red,
he should
probably use a moisturiser
but don't tell anyone he said that
to nobody in particular   anyone
who will listen, he's

ahead
of schedule with time
on his mind, going as slow
as he can, and most

of all
he wonders
why it is the CCTV camera
on the long pole outside
the massive police complex
on Paisley Road West
is always looking out towards
the trees in the park, it sometimes
swivels a click to the left   he wonders
if maybe the operator is
a bird watcher and someday soon
he's going to stop and go right on in
and ask, yes, someday soon
he's going to stop, and ask

Acknowledgements

Thanks are due to the editors of the following publications where some of these poems were first published: *The North, Look Up Glasgow* (Freight Books, 2013), *Edible Transmitters* (Bibliotheca Universalis, Romania, 2014), *Gutter, New Writing Scotland 32: Songs of Other Places, Glasgow Review of Books, Mistress Quickly's Bed, The Herald, Poetry Salzburg Review (Austria), Poetry Super Highway (USA), Scottish Poetry Library Best 20 Poems of 2014 online anthology, Northwords Now, New Writing Scotland 35: She Said He Said I Said, Mind the Time* (Nutmeg, 2017), *Nutmeg, Causeway/Cabhsair 10.2, Glasgow: Justice/Just is* (Seahorse Publications, 2019).